Lizards on the Wall

by Ken and Debby Buchanan

Illustrated by Betty Schweitzer-Johnson

Harbinger House

TUCSON

*To my parents, for teaching me to know
the desert—to see its life forms
with my heart and to hear its
ancient voices with my soul.*

D.B.

HARBINGER HOUSE, INC.
Tucson, Arizona
Copyright © 1992 by Ken and Debby Buchanan
Illustrations copyright © 1992 by Betty Schweitzer-Johnson

Printed in the United States of America
10 9 8 7 6 5 4 3 2 1

Library of Congress Cataloging-in-Publication Data

Buchanan, Ken.
Lizards on the wall / Ken and Debby Buchanan : illustrated by
Betty Schweitzer-Johnson.
p. cm.
Summary: An observer describes the nightly battle between the
insects in the room and the pair of lizards cavorting on the wall,
ISBN 0-943173-77-9 : $12.95
1. Lizards—Juvenile poetry. 2. Children's poetry. American.
[1. Lizards—Poetry. 2. American poetry.]   I. Buchanan, Debby,
1952–   .   II. Schweitzer-Johnson, Betty, 1950– ill.   III. title.
PS3552.U327L59   1992
811 ' .54—dc20   92-13664

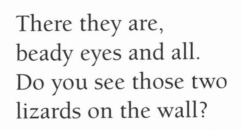

There they are,
beady eyes and all.
Do you see those two
lizards on the wall?

You'll find them there
all through the night
munching on bugs
in the pale moonlight.

I lie and watch them
from my bed
as they face each other
with bobbing heads.

I watch and laugh
as they zig and zag
and run around
playing games of tag.

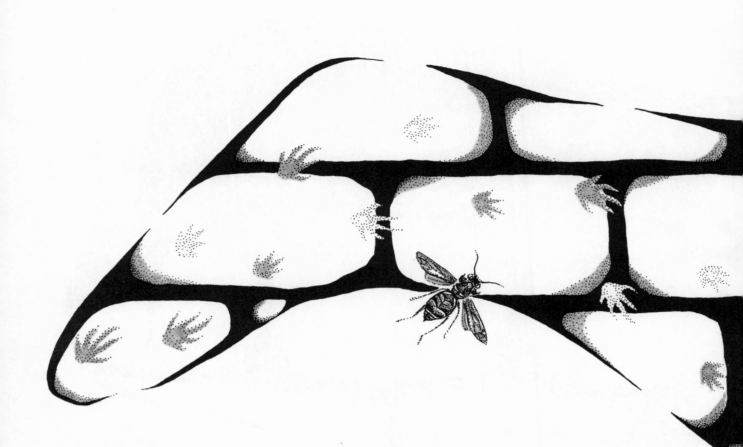

I can even hear their tiny claws
scratching as they crawl.
It's amazing how they skitter
across the dry adobe wall.

They roam like mighty hunters,
living wild and free.
They need to fill their bellies
just like you and me.

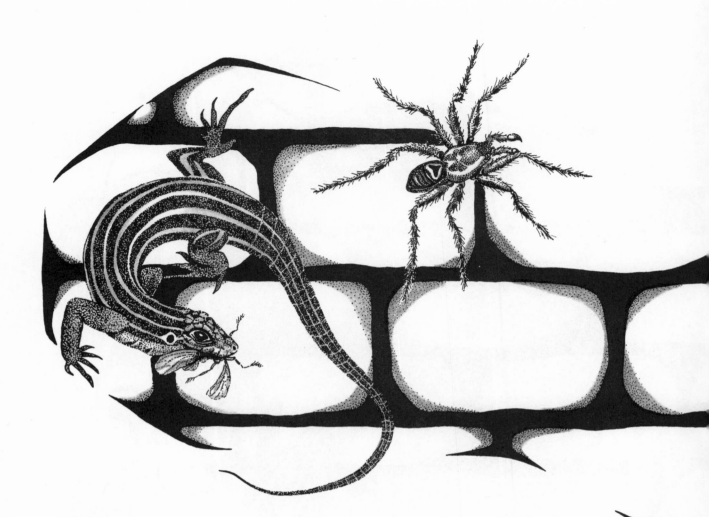

So . . .
striking with a swiftness
that takes my breath away,
they gobble bugs and spiders,
their very favorite prey.

Even the sinister scorpion
is no match for them.

One quick bite, done just right,
severs that terrible tail
and ends the fight!

The once fearsome beast
becomes just another
late-night feast.

Neither lizard on the wall
has ever been my pet.
And if I tried to catch one
he'd run away, I'll bet.

No . . .
I've never stroked their tiny heads,
nor taken them for a walk.
I've never tried to teach them tricks
like how to sit or talk.

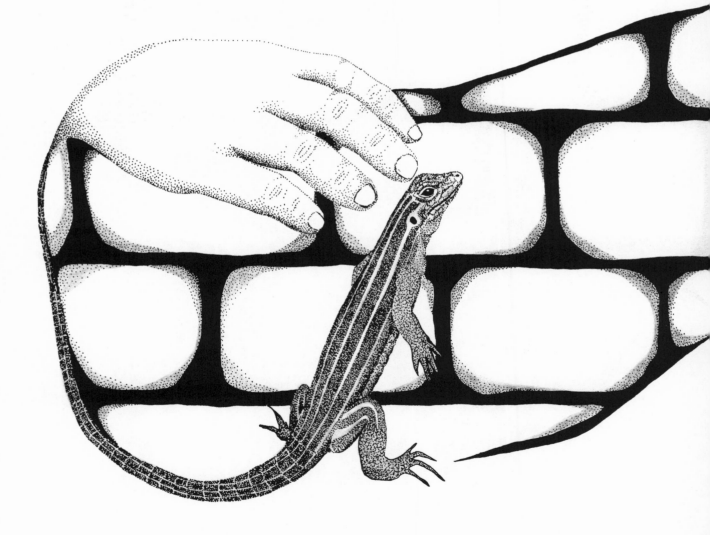

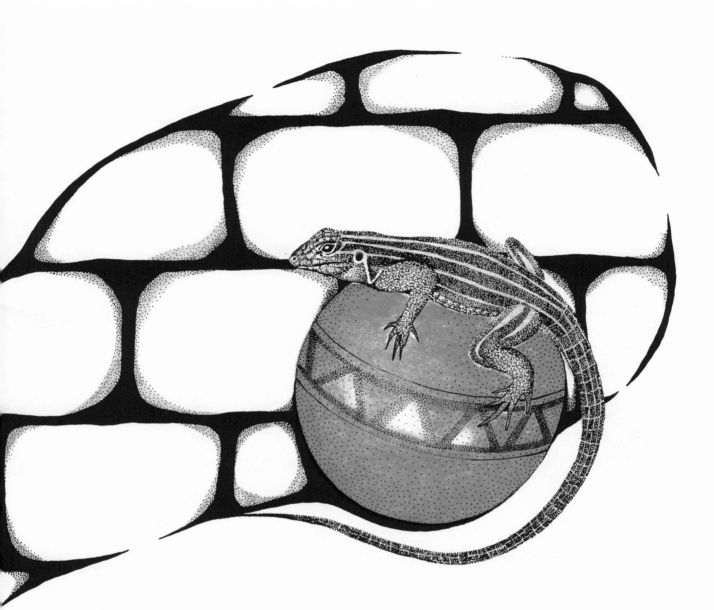

But they *are* my friends,
as you can see,
and when night begins
I know where they'll be . . .

They'll be eating up
those pesky things
that usually
eat me!

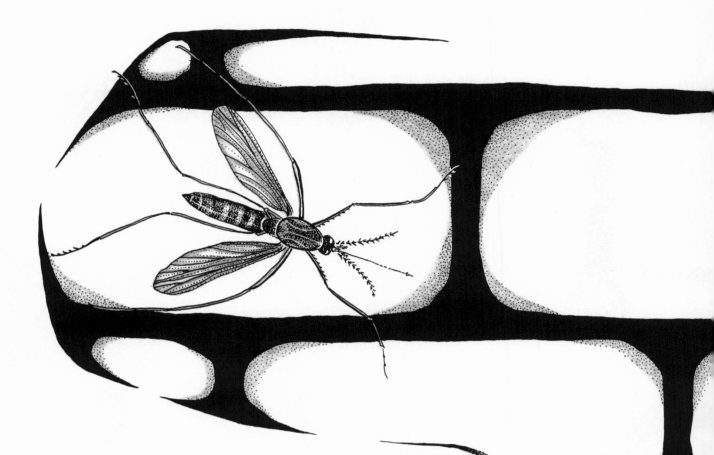

A buzzing mosquito
loose in my room,
sooner or later
will meet his doom.

Soldier ants
scouting at night
will become lizard dinner,
and that's all right.

Gnats and flies
that sting and bite
are cheerfully eaten
throughout the night.

Yes . . .
those lizards can see everything
with their flashing, little, dark eyes,

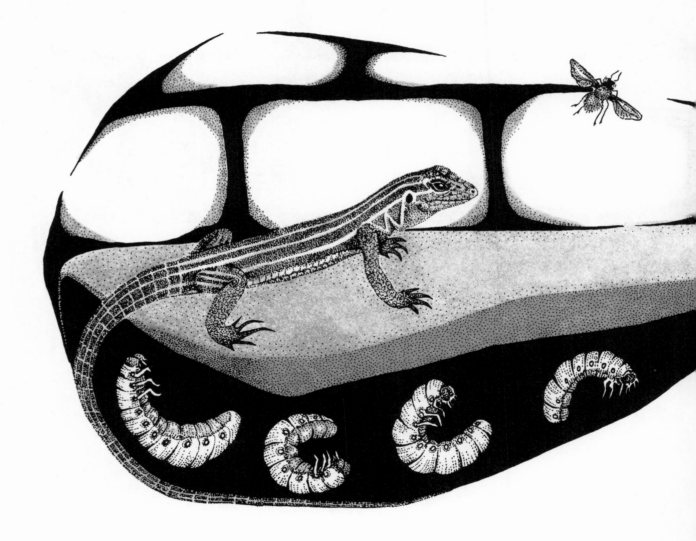

from the slowest crawling caterpillar,
to the fastest flight of a fly.

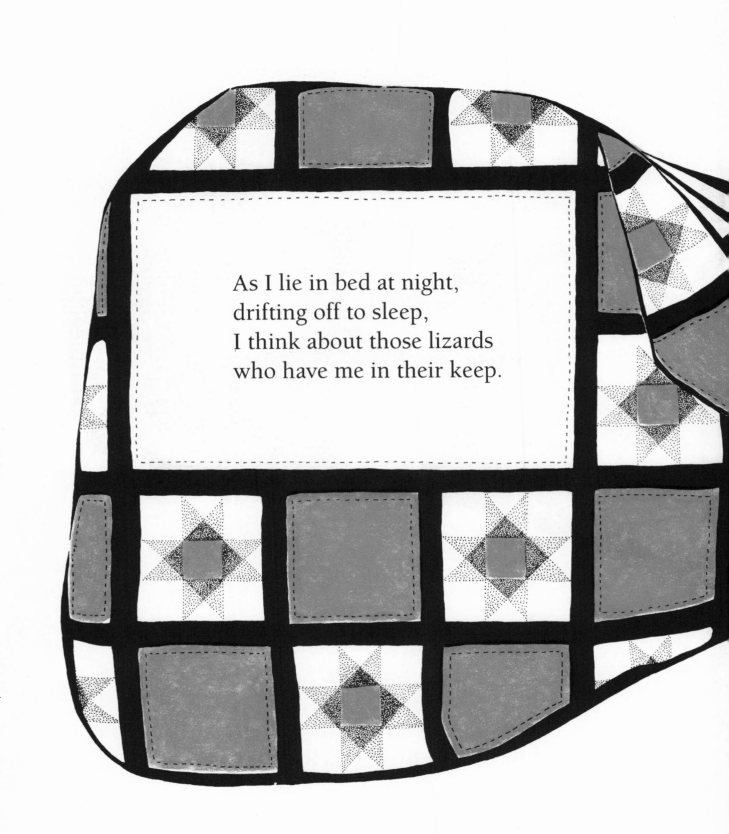

As I lie in bed at night,
drifting off to sleep,
I think about those lizards
who have me in their keep.

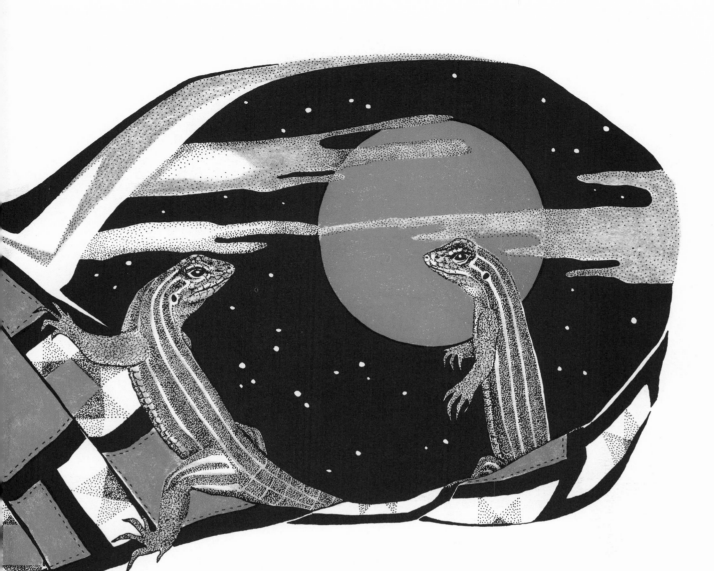

And I know that I am lucky
to have the company
of two such lively lizards
who are more than friends to me.

In fact . . .
I'm not ashamed
to tell you at all,
I love those two
lizards on the wall!